Introduction

The Museum of Costume at the Assembly Rooms, Bath was opened on 23rd May 1963. It was founded by Mrs Doris Langley Moore, OBE, the author and costume historian, whose internationally famous collection provided the basis for the Museum.

Mrs Moore began to form her private collection as a young woman in the 1920's and it quickly grew in succeeding years. By 1950 she had announced her intention of one day establishing a museum and her collection was, for a time, exhibited at Eridge Castle in Kent and at the Brighton Pavilion. The search for a permanent home, however, coincided with the restoration of the Bath Assembly Rooms which had been seriously damaged during the Second World War. It was decided to offer part of the premises to Mrs Moore for the display and storage of her collection and she generously bequeathed it to the City. Since then the Museum has been enriched by many other donations and loans and it is now one of the largest and most comprehensive collections of costume in the world. Until her retirement in 1974 Mrs Moore maintained close links with the Museum as its Honorary Adviser.

The Museum of Costume is housed on the lower ground floor of the Assembly Rooms, a fine eighteenth-century building designed by John Wood the Younger, one of Bath's most eminent architects. The Rooms were opened in 1771 to provide new facilities for the City's public entertainments – such as balls, assemblies and concerts – and for the next fifty years they were the centre of fashion in the West of England. After about 1820 Bath's popularity declined as a leading fashionable resort and the Rooms began to lose their original importance, eventually falling into disuse and disrepair in the present century. German incendiary bombs gutted the interior in 1942 and it was not until 1958 that a major programme of renovation was put in hand. The Rooms are owned by the National Trust but are leased to Bath City Council which is responsible for their maintenance and management. When, in 1975, Mr Kenneth Levy generously donated a sum of money for their redecoration the National Trust and City Council decided to embark on a joint scheme which had two main objectives. Firstly, the restoration of the interior and of the entrance area, secondly the reorganisation of the lower ground floor to accommodate a new Museum of Costume with improved layout and air conditioning.

The new Museum was designed by the City Architect, Roy Worskett, and the displays were set up by Myra Mines, the Chief Costume Assistant; it was opened by HRH the Princess Margaret, Countess of Snowdon in July 1979.

The earliest items in the Museum's collections date from the late – sixteenth century and there is a rare example of a woman's dress of the 1660's, but the majority of exhibits range from the early-eighteenth century to the present day. There are, in fact, very few garments which survive before the eighteenth century because textiles are extremely fragile; they will disintegrate with prolonged exposure to dust and daylight (and this is why the lighting in the Museum is reduced to the lowest level possible). The collections include the work of most leading haute couturiers of the present century and they are kept up to date with the annual addition of the 'Clothes of the Year' selected by an eminent fashion writer.

Most of the clothes on display are examples of fashionable dress; more ordinary and working garments tend not to survive in any number because they were often in use until they wore out and were not usually preserved for sentimental reasons (as were Wedding and Court dresses or Christening robes). Other types of costume, such as uniforms, theatrical and regional dress are also beyond the scope of the Museum. Nevertheless, it continues to add to its reserve collections with the aim of assembling as extensive a record as possible of the changing fashions of the past. About one tenth of the collection is on display at any one time which allows the exhibits to be changed at regular intervals and also 'rests' many of the costumes. The purpose of this brochure is to provide the visitor with a guide to the main changes in fashionable styles, illustrated by examples from the Museum of Costume's collections, and to describe some of the accessories to dress and other items that were worn and used. It is not, however, a catalogue of the exhibits and, because the displays are altered periodically, some of the costumes illustrated here may not always be on view. The arrangement of the brochure follows the layout of the Museum and the costumes are shown in chronological sequence.

The Museum would like to express its gratitude to all the donors of items featured in this brochure.

Displays at the Museum of Costume.

Fashion

It is sometimes difficult to associate the idea of fashion with clothes of the past. In itself fashion seems to be essentially modern, concerned with the present moment or the very near future; but at the same time, it is a continuously evolving process and almost every new style has developed from one already established. The history of costume is therefore a record of changing fashion and fashion itself consists in new or different ways of presenting the human figure.

Clothes can be used to disguise or emphasise the natural contours of the body and a different appearance can be created by enlarging one area or diminishing another.

In the mid-nineteenth century, for example, the 'hour-glass' figure was fashionable for women: waists were made smaller by tightly-laced corsets and the hips were enlarged by swelling skirts. By contrast, women of the 1920's emulated a boyish figure (a flat bust, no waist and slim hips) and wore tube-like shapeless dresses to camouflage their curves. The arrangement of the hair and accessories to dress can also produce very different effects.

Ideals of beauty and the fashionable silhouette altered in each period and were influenced not only by the desire for change or something new but also by contemporary ideas and current artistic taste. Women's clothes of the later-nineteenth century, for instance, were elaborate and restricting but they were, in part, an expression of the widespread taste for lavish ornament and also of the dependent status of women at that period.

Fashion is very rarely influenced by what is practical or comfortable and many examples in the Museum of Costume demonstrate this point (up to and including the present day). On the whole, however, men's clothes have always tended to be more utilitarian than women's, probably because of their more active life-style until quite recent times.

Although men's and women's clothes are basically different the same fashionable trends are often discernible in both. In the 1830's men's coats had well-defined waists with fairly full skirts and the shoulder-seam was slightly dropped, producing a silhouette which was not unlike that of the fashionable woman's. These features can be seen in the fashion plates of the period.

Fashion, as a rule is a spontaneous reaction and new styles reflect changes in mood or the social and economic climate. Fashion designers are usually quick to detect and anticipate these changes and they produce clothes which they think people will want to wear as a result of them. They can direct the course of fashion but it is not usual, contrary to what is often supposed, for designers to dictate it; it is difficult to impose a new fashion on men and women if they genuinely do not like it (and there are many ideas which have failed).

Before the mid-nineteenth century very few tailors or dressmakers were known by name and they were considered as craftsmen rather than artists in their own right; but the work of Charles Frederick Worth established the profession of the haute couturier and his was one of the first great fashion houses. News of changing styles was also limited in earlier periods and fashion magazines only began to appear regularly at the end of the eighteenth century. Until then, news was spread by letter or by word of mouth and small dolls dressed in fashionable clothes were often circulated. A rare eighteenth-century example is on display in the Museum.

Fashions from the Belle Assemblée 1847.

Fashions from the Mercure des Salons 1830.

2

17th & 18th Century Fashion

In this and the following section on **Textiles and Embroidery** garments and dress accessories of the seventeenth and eighteenth century are described; this section deals with the fashionable styles, the next with materials and decoration.

The Museum of Costume is fortunate in having a complete costume from the seventeenth century and this silver tissue dress of the 1660's is a rare example of women's fashion in the English Restoration period.

It was probably intended for Court or formal wear because the material (a silk woven with a metal thread) is very fine and the bodice is cut with a low neck opening and short sleeves. It was usual for the bodice and skirt to be separate at this date and the bodice was laced at the back. The fashionable line was long and rigid, there was heavy boning and stiffening in the bodice and the waist dipped to a point at the centre front. The round skirt is pleated at the waist but the front panel is straight and flat. A white linen shift with long, full sleeves was worn beneath the dress. The wide neck line, which is almost off the shoulder, is trimmed with a deep collar of Venetian needlepoint lace and the bodice and skirt are decorated with applied bands of lace. The hair was arranged in loose curls or ringlets over the ears but drawn into a tight bun at the back of the head.

At the same period men's clothes settled into a new fashion for a three-piece suit consisting of a coat,

(Above) Coat of brown cloth embroidered in silver 1720-30. (Right) Dress of silver tissue 1660-70.

waistcoat and knee breeches and the long, curled periwig was adopted. Men also wore lace which was displayed at the neck and wrists. It was a fashionable but very expensive item, James II for example, paid £36.10s. for a cravat to wear at his coronation in 1685.

The early-eighteenth century coat was knee length with long vents in the side and back seams; these allowed the hilt and blade of the sword – an essential accessory to the dress of a gentleman – to pass through the garment. Extra fabric was pleated into these vents to give a full-skirted effect. The coat had no collar and there were buttons from neck to hem, but it was normally only fastened at the waist. There were deep, flapped pockets at hip level and the sleeves had deep wide cuffs. One of the finest examples of a cloth coat known to exist from around 1720 is in the Museum of Costume and it was made for the third Sir Thomas Kirkpatrick when he was fifteen or sixteen years old. The brown woollen cloth is lavishly embroidered with silver and a pair of matching brown knitted silk stockings with silver embroidery also survive. Men's stockings at this date were rolled up over the lower edge of the knee breeches which were fairly loose fitting. The waistcoat was cut on similar lines to the coat but was a few inches shorter; it was usually, though not always, sleeveless and was often made in a contrasting colour and material to the coat. The white linen shirt had a deep neckband round which was folded the neckcloth or cravat, tied end-over-end at the front.

The fashionable style of wig until about 1730 was the 'full-bottomed' a long, curled wig with a centre parting. Men cropped their own hair short or shaved their heads to ensure a closer, more comfortable fit for the wig. For informal wear, at home, the wig was replaced by a soft cap called a night cap or morning cap and it was generally worn with a long, loose gown or easy indoor coat.

The gown was known by a variety of names such as dressing gown, night gown, morning gown or India gown, but all refer to an unfitted garment cut on simple lines, not unlike a modern dressing gown. It was loosely wrapped over the shirt and waistcoat when the coat was removed. An alternative style, sometimes called a banyan, was more tailored, with closer fitting sleeves and a front fastening like a coat.

Although dressing gowns were strictly informal it appears that men wore them in the Pump Room at Bath in the early-eighteenth century. Richard Nash, the Master of Ceremonies, however, disapproved of the custom and his Rules for Polite Behaviour in 1742 stated 'that Gentlemen of Fashion never appearing in a morning before the Ladies in Gowns and Caps shew Breeding and Respect', (the 'gowns' and 'caps' here referring to the men's morning gowns and morning caps).

Another of Nash's 'rules' was to forbid ladies to wear aprons at evening balls and assemblies. Aprons had become a fashionable and very decorative accessory to women's dress but they were not correct with the most formal dress for evening or Court occasions. When the Duchess of Queensberry appeared at a ball in the Assembly Rooms in an apron of finest lace (said to be worth several hundred guineas) Nash pulled it off her. At other times of the day the apron was perfectly correct and it was worn throughout the eighteenth century.

Pink damask dressing gown and cap c.1720; blue damask banyan c.1750.

Green damask dress 1747, with white embroidered muslin apron.

There were several different styles of women's gowns during the century. Some were open at the front in both the bodice and skirt, others were open only in the skirt, and the so-called 'round gown' was completely closed.

A separate bodice and skirt was another but less usual variation. The open-fronted gown was worn over an underskirt or 'petticoat' which could either match or contrast with the gown and the opening between the front edges of the bodice was filled in with a triangular panel called the stomacher (which was often given decorative treatment).

Beneath the gown the long, sleeved shift, a pair of stays (or corset) and a hoop petticoat were worn. Stout linen petticoats reinforced with cane hoops gave the skirt its fashionable bell shape until the 1730's; the skirt then flattened at the back and front and extended at the sides to become almost rectangular in the late 1740's.

Indoor's, fine white linen caps or lace head-dresses were customary wear for all women while the wide-brimmed straw hat was worn out of doors, in the country or garden.

Ladies and gentlemen attending Court functions in the eighteenth century were expected to be richly dressed. Not only were the finest and most expensive silks chosen for suits and dresses, they were also further decorated with embroidery and applied gold and silver lace or braid. There are several examples of ladies' Court dresses in the Museum and two are particularly fine: one, in a brocaded silk dating from around 1745 and the other, of an embroidered silk, said to have been worn at the Court of George III in 1761 (details of these appear on page 11). Both dresses have very wide hoops or 'paniers' (basket-like supports worn over the hips) which reached their most exaggerated shape in about 1750 and then subsided. Although the hoop petticoat passed out of fashionable use in the 1750's it continued to be worn with Court dress until the end of the century. Another feature of some Court dresses was a long train which could be carried over one arm for walking.

By the late 1750's women's dresses had taken on a new appearance. Once hoops were abandoned skirts looked softer and narrower, falling into more graceful folds. There was a much lighter character in the patterning of dress silks with a preference for smaller floral motifs and more delicate decoration. Ruched or pleated trimmings were added to the front edges of the gown and flounces to the hem of the petticoat. Triple-tiered ruffles were attached to the elbow-length sleeves and the stomacher was highly decorated. It became fashionable to leave off the cap and wear instead a small ornament of ribbon, lace or feathers on the head.

After the 1730's the shape of the male suit also began to change. The width in the coat skirts was gradually reduced to achieve a slimmer fit; at the same time the front edges of the coat began to curve back at the sides revealing more of the waistcoat and knee breeches. In turn, more attention was paid to the cut of these garments – the waistcoat became narrower and shorter and breeches much tighter. By 1760 the set of clothes presented a much longer and more slender line. Suits for dress wear were made from silks and velvets or fine woollen cloth which might be embroidered in coloured silks or gold and silver thread. They were worn with white knitted silk or cotton stockings (now pulled up under the lower edge of the breeches) and buckled shoes. Boots were confined to outdoor and country wear.

Man's suit of Genoa velvet c.1755 and woman's brocaded silk dress 1750-60.

Embroidered Court dress and matching shoes 1761.

In the 1740's the stock, a neckcloth pleated or gathered into a band that fastened at the back of the neck, became a popular alternative to the cravat. The 'tie' or 'bag' wig was now fashionable with formal dress, it was a shorter wig with the hair rolled in curls over the ears and the tail at the back enclosed in a black silk bag (finished with a bow at the nape of the neck). The wig was dressed with a mixture of pomatum (grease) and fine powder. Most men in England wore wigs in the mid-eighteenth century but some wore their own hair dressed to look like a wig. All men were clean shaven at this time.

The arrangement of women's hair altered during the 1760's, gradually becoming looser and fuller; by the 1770's the head was dressed very high and the hair was built up over a pad while being greased and powdered.

The heroine of Fanny Burney's novel **Evelina** (1778) described the experience when she wrote 'I have just had my hair dressed. You can't think how oddly my head feels; full of powder and black pins, and a great *cushion* on the top of it.

I believe you would hardly know me, for my face looks quite different to what it did before my hair was dressed. When I shall be able to make use of a comb for myself I cannot tell, for my hair is so much entangled, *frizled* they call it, that I fear it will be very difficult'.

Perhaps the most popular style of women's dress in the eighteenth century was the sack-back gown, fashionable until the 1770's. Its distinctive feature was a loose back falling staight from the shoulders in two double box pleats. The sack was usually open at the centre front and worn with a stomacher and matching petticoat. When made for more formal occasions the back could be lengthened into a short train and the gown was extensively trimmed (often with gold or silver lace). Plainer versions of the sack were produced for ordinary wear but there was a general preference for ornament. Dress silks woven in stripes interspersed with small sprays of flowers were particularly favoured.

The 1780's and 1790's saw a complete change of mood and the emergence of new styles of dress for both men and women. The taste for rich and formal dress silks, elaborate embroidery and a profusion of lace gave way to a liking for simpler, lighter and more informal clothes. In the 1780's light-weight cottons and linens imported from the East were becoming fashionable for women's dresses and the softer texture of these materials affected the cut and shape of the gown. The waistline began to rise and skirts

Brocaded silk sack-back dress 1760-70.

were softly pleated with an increased fullness at the back. Cross-over bodices or bodices filled in with a white muslin neck-handkerchief were especially fashionable by the 1790's. Silks continued to be worn but those with a light, almost papery texture were preferred; the most popular dress material, however, was rapidly becoming muslin (a general term for thin and finely-woven cotton fabrics). Muslins could be plain, printed, embroidered or woven with a small design.

By 1780 the towering hair arrangements began to subside, eventually falling into a mass of loose curls which were intended to look as natural as possible. Large caps, to accommodate the size of the head, and broad-brimmed straw hats trimmed with flowers or feathers were fashionable dress accessories.

The open-fronted gown and petticoat were worn until the end of the century but after the 1770's the sack-back passed out of fashion and the closed bodice became normal. A pair of stays was still customary beneath the gown but the shape was less rigid than in previous decades. The preference for simpler, more countrified clothes was, to some extent, influenced by the outbreak of the French Revolution in 1789. In following years anything that seemed aristocratic or ostentatious went out of favour, in particular, very formal clothes and precious jewellery. Men began to discard lace wrist ruffles and elaborate shoe-buckles and adopted a plainer form of dress for daytime wear. Woollen cloth in sober colours was used for most coats and breeches while silks, with woven or embroidered patterns, were now confined to the most formal dress. The informal riding coat, with a turned-down collar, began to be worn in town and there was an air of ease and comfort in the male suit. The waistcoat had shortened to waist level by 1780 and could have a double- or single-breasted fastening and a small stand collar. Breeches were rather longer and tighter fitting, sometimes made in a more pliable material than cloth, such as a jersey-weave stockinet; often they did not match the coat or waistcoat and light colours were fashionable. A small pocket in the waistband held the watch from which hung a ribbon or chain with a pair of fob seals attached (pendant seals bearing a coat of arms or other device were essential for letters or business purposes and were usually carried on the person).

The cravat returned to fashion and consisted of a large square of lawn or muslin, folded cornerwise into a band and wrapped round the neck to tie in a knot or bow at the front. In the 1790's wigs disappeared and only the more conservative or elderly men continued to use powder. Fashionable young men wore their own hair cut short and in its natural state.

Man's cream cloth coat and breeches 1780-90; woman's printed muslin dress 1780-90.

Man's suit of pinstripe corded silk c.1795; woman's gold silk dress with cream hand-painted petticoat 1795-1800.

Textiles & Embroidery

Until comparatively recent times, all garments were made of cloth woven from natural fibres. It was not until the late-nineteenth century that experiments were successful in producing artificial silk and most of the other man-made fibres so widely used today date from only just before and after the Second World War.

The four main natural fibres used for clothing until the second half of the twentieth century were wool, silk, linen and cotton. Wool and silk are animal fibres while linen and cotton are vegetable fibres and the use of all four goes back to the earliest times.

Wool was probably the first fibre to be used for spinning and weaving into fabric for the making of clothes. It was readily available throughout most parts of the world and it produced a material which was both adaptable and practical. Different species of sheep yield fibres of varying lengths, texture and colour and plain woollen cloths may range from the softest and lightest weights to the coarsest, thickest and heaviest of materials.

Silk, from the long filament produced by the secretion of the silkworm, has always been the costliest and most luxurious of the natural fibres. The original centres for the cultivation and weaving of silk were in Asia but in the early mediaeval period raw silk was imported into Europe and woven into fine cloths there. Italy was the centre of the silk weaving industry in Europe in the Middle Ages.

Man's waistcoat of gold tissue brocaded in coloured silks, chenille and silver thread 1765-70.

Linen fabric is produced from the stalk of the flax plant and it seems originally to have been cultivated for this purpose in Egypt, one of the richest agricultural areas of the world. From the evidence of archaeological excavations it was used for clothing in very early periods and there are, of course, many references to linen in the Bible.

Cotton, from the cotton plant, is one of the most widely used and versatile textile fabrics although it did not become fashionable in European dress until the late-seventeenth century. For thousands of years cotton was cultivated in India, Egypt and China, later it reached the Mediterranean countries and finally North America became the greatest centre of production.

Until the late-eighteenth century most outer garments for men and women in Europe were made of either woollen cloth or silk. Because of its delicacy and cost, silk always tended to be reserved for more formal dress and in some periods its use was restricted to members of the middle and upper classes. Women often bequeathed their best silk gowns to relatives or servants in their wills or left them to the Church to be made into ecclesiastical vestments or furnishings. During the early-eighteenth century a native silk industry flourished in Spitalfields in London but fine dress silks continued to be imported from France or Italy.

In the mediaeval period the best quality woollen cloths were processed in Italy and the Low Countries, woven mainly from wool imported from England; later England herself became a manufacturer of woollen cloth. The English term 'broadcloth' refers to the best cloth which was closely woven with a lustrous nap and had a soft drape; this was used for fashionable male and female dress and it was expensive.

Linen is the oldest material to have been used for undergarments and the word, in fact, became synonymous with underclothing. Even in the nineteenth century, when cotton was widely used, fine linen was considered the better and socially more correct fabric for underwear. It is particularly suitable to wear next to the skin because its texture is smooth and cool and it absorbs moisture. It also washes well and for centuries provided a hygienic layer (which could be laundered frequently) between the outer garments and the skin. The basic undergarments, until the end of the nineteenth century, were a long-sleeved linen shirt for men and a long shift or chemise, with sleeves, for women.

From a very early period embroidery was used not only as a form of decoration but also as a means of strengthening garments (for example by reinforcing seams or areas exposed to hard wear). Men's shirts of the sixteenth century illustrate this point in the use of the fashionable blackwork embroidery of the time. The parts of the shirt which were visible at the neck, wrists and centre-front opening were given decorative treatment and these embroidered areas made an important contribution to the general effect of the whole costume; but it is also likely that the embroidery had a practical application in helping disguise the inevitable soiling of white linen at neck and wrists. Blackwork appears to have been Arabic in origin and spread from Spain to

Woman's doublet of linen embroidered in coloured silks and metal thread 1610-20.

Man's white linen shirt embroidered in black thread 1600-10.

England before the beginning of the sixteenth century.
The early designs were geometrical in character but in
England they soon became transformed into very
naturalistic motifs of flowers, animals and insects.
A particularly fine example of a man's shirt in the Museum of
Costume illustrates the Elizabethan delight in flowers and the
countryside with its interlacing pattern of coiling stems, roses, oak
leaves, insects and birds.
The English tradition for fine embroidery is an old one, going back to
at least the thirteenth century. Patterned silk fabrics (that is, with a
woven or brocaded pattern) were expensive because England was so far
from the silk-weaving centres in Europe and it is possible that this
encouraged the development of elaborate embroidery in this country, since
highly-decorated silks or other cloths were required for ecclesiastical, Court or
ceremonial wear.
In the late-sixteenth and early-seventeenth centuries there was a fashionable
emphasis on the surface decoration of clothes, and embroidery in brightly-coloured
silks and metal thread was popular. A number of the embroidered jackets or doublets
that were an established fashion throughout the reigns of Elizabeth and James I have
survived and the examples in this Museum show the techniques of both blackwork and silk
embroidery with gold and silver thread with spangles. Most of these were worked on linen.
During this and later periods embroidery was done both by amateurs at home and by
professionals organised on similar lines to the tailors. Some of the outstanding examples of
embroidered garments that still exist are likely to have been the work of professional
embroiderers.
During the eighteenth century embroidery continued to decorate dress and dress accessories such as
pockets, aprons, gloves and shoes and it was often considered essential for the most formal clothes.
The stomacher (a detachable triangular panel used to fill in the bodice of an open-fronted gown),
for instance, was frequently lavishly embroidered and for very special occasions was also set with precious
stones.
Men's coats and waistcoats were similarly treated and embroidery could be applied to garments made of both
silks and woollen cloths. Waistcoats for dress wear were especially fine; the most formal were almost always
made in silk, either plain or patterned with the further addition of embroidery. A typical example (illustrated on
page 8) is of silk woven with a gold thread and a brocaded floral pattern. The front edges and pocket flaps are
brocaded in coloured silks and the buttons have been made to match.

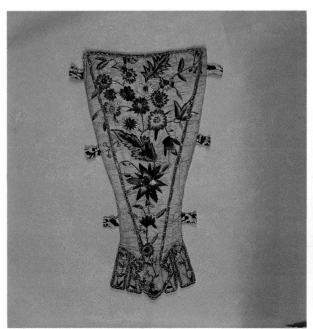

Woman's stomacher of embroidered yellow silk c.1740.

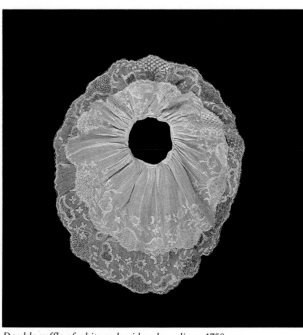

Double ruffle of white embroidered muslin, c.1750.

Another form of embroidery fashionable during the eighteenth century was whitework. Fine white lawn or muslin caps, aprons, handkerchiefs and sleeve ruffles were often embroidered in white thread in delicate, naturalistic floral patterns, sometimes with the addition of decorative fillings. Whitework could be worn as an alternative to lace. In the last two decades of the century fine linens and cottons began to replace silk for women's dresses and white embroidered garments became increasingly fashionable.

A great variety of patterned silks were available to men and women in England in the eighteenth century and these were produced both at home and abroad.

A Court dress of around 1745 in the Museum of Costume is an example of an Italian silk woven or brocaded in gold with a coloured floral pattern, part of which is executed in a velvet technique giving the fabric a depth and variety of surface texture apart from its general richness.

Often, however, it was not considered enough to wear a brocaded silk at court and some of the finest dresses were embroidered all over (the handwork representing a considerable amount of time, skill and expense). It is clear from eighteenth-century letters of Mary Delany, whose detailed descriptions of contemporary fashion are an invaluable source of information, that Court dress was taken very seriously and it undoubtedly contributed to the magnificent spectacle that these occasions must have presented. Great use was made of gold and silver in the clothes and Mrs Delany rarely mentions a Court dress which is not trimmed, embroidered or woven with metal thread. A magnificent example of around 1761 on display in the Museum bears out the contemporary descriptions of Court dress and demonstrates the use of metal thread and spangles with coloured silks. Details of these two dresses illustrate the difference between a brocaded and an embroidered silk (both of them skilled techniques): the first has a pattern woven into the fabric while the second has the decoration applied to the surface of it.

Detail of embroidered Court dress 1761.

Detail of brocaded silk Court dress c.1745.

Accessories

Accessories to dress include items which may be worn or carried to complete an outfit or fulfil some useful purpose. Hats, shoes and gloves, for example, are garments which are often an integral part of a whole costume while objects such as fans, aprons, bags and purses can be both functional and decorative.

The fan was one of the most important and fashionable accessories to women's dress in the eighteenth century. Its original purpose (since the earliest periods in history) was to cool the face and this was still a consideration at the crowded evening assemblies that were a part of eighteenth-century social life. The decorative nature of its design, however, was a significant feature and some of the most beautiful fans were produced at this period. Many were folding fans with a painted paper or skin leaf mounted on sticks of wood, ivory, tortoiseshell, mother-of-pearl, horn or bone. The sticks were often carved, pierced, painted or gilded and the guards (the outer sticks protecting the fan when closed) were further decorated. Most of the painted designs were of classical, mythological or biblical scenes and sometimes historical events were featured. After about 1720 paper leaves printed with maps, almanacks, games or commemorative themes were popular. Fan leaves might also be made of silk gauze, painted or embroidered with spangles. The alternative type of fan was the brisé fan which, instead of having an attached leaf, consisted of a series of tapered, overlapping sticks joined along the outer edge by a fine silk ribbon threaded through. Again, many of these were delicately carved in a variety of materials and some of the finest were of ivory and tortoiseshell imported from the East; they could also be painted.

Apron of embroidered yellow silk 1730-40.

A selection of eighteenth-century fans.

Pair of pockets in quilted and embroidered green silk c.1740.

Blue satin shoe c.1750; pair of paste and metal shoe buckles in own box c.1750.

Aprons, though practical in origin, had become a decorative indoor accessory in the eighteenth century and fashionable examples were elaborately embroidered. They continued to be worn in the nineteenth century.

Women's shoes in the eighteenth century were often made to match the dress and uppers of silk or other cloth were more usual than leather until the 1780's (but shoes for travelling or walking and men's footwear were made in leather). Satins and brocaded and embroidered silks were fashionable with leather soles and were made entirely by hand. Heels on shoes did not emerge until around 1600; by the eighteenth century they were moderately high and the toe was rounded or pointed. Overshoes or 'pattens' (sometimes made to match) gave the shoe additional protection out of doors.

Both men's and women's shoes fastened with buckles which secured the two overlapping straps over the instep. Buckles were completely removeable and interchangeable. Until the last two decades of the century they were the focal point of footwear, altering shape according to fashion and made with care and imagination. They were, in fact, regarded as items of jewellery, they were often given as presents and were kept in satin-lined cases. Silver was the most usual metal used but gold, pinchbeck and steel were also worn. In the 1740's buckles were fashionably set with precious stones, paste, marcasites or real diamonds and became rather larger. They reached their greatest size in the 1770's but by the 1790's passed out of fashion.

Cloth uppers continued in use for shoes and boots for dress wear in the nineteenth century. Black or white satin heelless pumps were fashionable from about 1830–1860 and heels were again general from the 1860's. Half-boots in satin were also worn and leather or stouter cloth tops were general for more practical wear.

Gloves were another accessory both functional and decorative. Sixteenth and seventeenth-century gloves, for example, were lavishly embroidered in coloured silks and metal thread, trimmed with fringe and ribbons. For formal wear, in the eighteenth century, women wore long (elbow-length) white kid gloves and these remained correct with evening dress well into the present century. During the nineteenth century white kid gloves were always worn at night but the length and type of fastening varied from time to time. Men also wore short white kid gloves with evening dress. Gloves were essential with outdoor dress for both men and women until after the Second World War and have continued to be worn with formal clothes.

Black and white silk mittens in openwork mesh (worked either by hand or machine) were a fashionable dress accessory for women in the 1830's and 1840's. They were again worn in the 1870's and 1880's and were revived in the early years of this century. Muffs were also used to keep the hands warm in the eighteenth and nineteenth centuries. Large ones were popular in the period 1790–1820.

Until recent times, hats have been important accessories to male and female costume. There is a very long tradition of covering the head both indoors and out; up to the end of the nineteenth century it was customary for married women to wear caps in the house and a number of examples, trimmed with lace, ribbons and embroidery are on display in the Museum's Millinery Section. Bonnets and hats were worn out of doors during the nineteenth century but bonnets were the more formal of the two until the 1890's. In the early years of the present century fasionable hats for women were very large and could be extensively trimmed with ornaments, artificial flowers or feathers (sometimes even a whole bird). The long hat pins with large heads date from this period.

The fashionable hat for men in the eighteenth century was three-cornered – turned up or 'cocked' on three sides. A flat, crescent-shaped hat with brim turned up at front and back was carried under the arm on formal occasions in the late-eighteenth century and this was called the 'chapeau bras'. It continued in use for Court wear for some time. The nineteenth-century top hat originated from the tall-crowned country or riding hat of the 1780's and this could be made in both black and cream. A version covered in black corded silk was made for evening wear and in 1835 a folding hat (with a metal spring in the crown) was invented. Bowler hats of hard felt were introduced for informal wear in the 1860's and two other soft felt hats known as the trilby and homburg were worn from the later-nineteenth century onwards. In the summer straw boaters and panama hats were alternatives to these more casual styles.

Hat of purple beaver trimmed with a stuffed pheasant c.1908.

Costume accessories 1900-20.

Babies' Clothes

Until the early-eighteenth century the practice of swaddling babies was prevalent in this country. For the first month to six weeks of its life a baby was tightly bound into a cocoon by a swaddling band which, it was believed, would protect its fragile limbs. By the 1740's the custom was being openly criticised but it did continue in some areas of Europe into the nineteenth century.

The basic undergarment for all babies was a shirt (which was also worn beneath swaddling bands) and it was usually made of fine linen and might be trimmed with openwork stitching or lace. By the eighteenth century, stays (a firm bodice) and a flannel petticoat were worn over this with napkins (called clouts) and a pilch (a flannel cloth put over the napkin at night). Sometimes a muslin petticoat came over these garments and then the frock. Caps were considered very important for both day and night wear; two were worn, a close fitting under cap and a more decorative outer one. Out of doors a shawl might be worn and after the 1830's long woollen cloaks with hoods became a usual fashion. Mittens and little boots and shoes were also worn. Elaborate versions of these garments were made for christenings and they were often beautifully embroidered. These items tended to be preserved for sentimental reasons and many survive in museums today. A particularly fine collection of babies' clothes from the seventeenth century may be seen in the Museum of Costume and these were probably part of a christening set which included a shirt, collars, short and long bibs, detachable sleeves, caps and a forehead piece worn under a cap. They are made of white linen embroidered with applied linen cord.

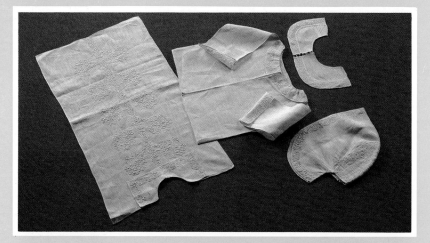

(Above) Seventeenth century babies' clothes.
(Right) White satin robe with silk embroidery, mid-eighteenth century.

A special robe was usually made for the christening and in the eighteenth century these were often made of white or cream satin trimmed with embroidery in the same coloured silk or silk braid and fringe. The robe opened at the centre front and had elbow-length sleeves with turn-back cuffs.

During the nineteenth century babies' christening robes and long gowns for special occasions were very elaborately embroidered and were displayed with pride. Gowns were made longer and fuller (the skirt often measuring more than a yard in length) and were influenced, to some extent, by the changing shapes of women's fashions.

The centre front panels of the bodice and skirt were enriched with white embroidery such as Ayrshire work or broderie anglaise. Ayrshire work – delicate white embroidery on muslin in raised satin stitch with decorative needlepoint fillings – was particulary fashionable from around 1830–1870; a slightly coarser type of embroidery or cut-work, called broderie anglaise, became popular after about 1850. At the end of the century insertions of lace and fine tucking were also added to babies' gowns.

Caps for indoor wear began to be discarded after the mid-nineteenth century but were always worn out of doors. There are a number of examples in the Museum illustrating the decorative treatment they were given. A number of eighteenth-century caps had insertions of lace, a popular form of which was needlepoint lace known as 'Hollie-point'. Lace was frequently used for trimming or for an entire cap in the nineteenth century and some were delicately knitted with the addition of coloured beads. Silk ribbon was another form of decoration.

White embroidered cap with insertion of Hollie-point lace, late-eighteenth century.

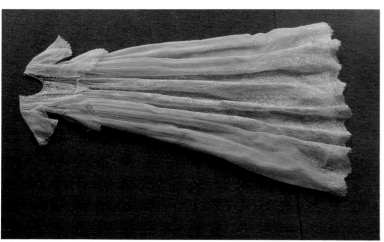

White embroidered christening robe, late-nineteenth century.

15

Jewellery

Jewellery, of precious metals and gemstones, has long been used as a means of adornment – not only decorating the clothes and person but also indicating social standing and financial status. Some items of jewellery may be both decorative and functional.

Brooches and pins, for example, are often used to secure a garment and shoe buckles of the seventeenth and eighteenth centuries were an indispensable method of fastening male and female footwear.

The usual areas for decoration have been the head and neck, wrists and hands. Some pieces of jewellery, however, may form a part of the costume – such as a head-dress – or be attached to a garment. The green paste stomacher buckle illustrated here is an instance; it dates from the mid-eighteenth century and matches a necklace of thirteen stones with a pendant. The buckle fastens with a pin and the necklace has loops at either end for ribbon ties. Also illustrated is a cross of white paste set in silver dating from the period c.1680–1720. Paste is a material originally produced to imitate diamonds but it soon came to be valued in its own right and appeared in other colours.

At the end of the eighteenth century, with the reaction against ostentation in dress, there was a fashion for jewellery made of less precious metals and stones. Pinchbeck, an imitation gold made from a copper and zinc alloy, was much liked as was cut steel. Marcasites (faceted crystals of iron pyrites) were also originally used to imitate diamonds.

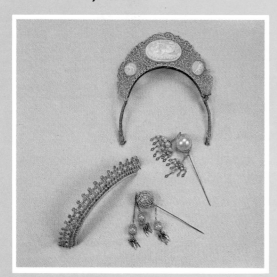

Tiaras and lappet pins 1800-50.

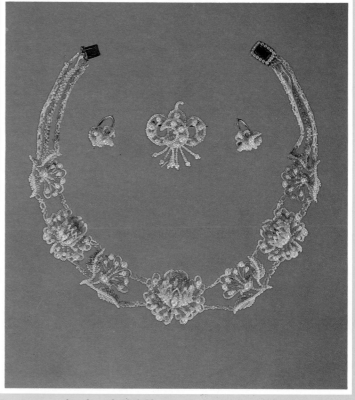

Demi-parure of seed pearls 1840-50.

Pearls have always been valued but in the early Victorian period small seed pearls were particularly fashionable, often threaded in narrow strings, loops and clusters. A matching set of necklace, earrings, and brooch dating from the 1840's has a design of flowers and foliage arranged in this way.

Mourning or memorial jewellery is usually associated with the Victorian era although it was worn at earlier times. Rings inscribed with initials or mottoes were frequently distributed amongst relatives and friends at funerals and by the nineteenth century brooches and lockets suitably decorated or inscribed in memory of a departed loved one were widely adopted. Favourite devices were funerary urns, weeping willow trees or doves and many of these were worked in hair. Black enamel, jet and dark wood were other materials often used.

Human hair became extremely popular for nineteenth-century jewellery and was used in different ways: sometimes it was employed as an embroidery thread; sometimes a lock was coiled or plaited and enclosed in a ring, locket or brooch; it could also be plaited or woven into much larger shapes. Drop-earings could be made from a lattice-work of hair and some were in fanciful shapes such as acorns or crosses. A large amount of hair could also be plaited into a rope and twisted for extra thickness to make a bracelet.

Ornaments for the head have been worn by women for formal wear in most periods. Tiaras of precious metal set with stones or cameos were fashionable in the early nineteenth century and by the 1830's hair ornaments with quivering, pendant decorations were worn with the elaborate hair arrangements of the period.

Costume jewellery, that is, jewellery which is not made in precious metal or set with real stones became popular with day clothes in the 1920's and 1930's and has remained a fashionable alternative since then.

Paste cross, c.1680-1720; paste stomacher buckle and necklace c.1750.

Bracelet, earrings and brooch of human hair 1850-70.

Mourning jewellery 1855-80.

Necklace and earrings of ruby paste 1960-70.

19th Century Fashion

The nineteenth century opened with a distinctive style of dress for women inspired by the Neo-Classical taste then prevalent in both the fine and decorative arts. Short-waisted gowns with long and softly-draped skirts in the lightest of materials that gently outlined the natural contours of the figure were almost universally adopted and remained in fashion for over a decade. The dresses were intended to imitate the draperies of Ancient Greek and Roman statues so that light-weight and light-coloured fabrics with only the most delicate decoration, in the classical style, were chosen.

Muslin proved to be the most suitable material, not only because it was soft and almost transparent but also because it could be easily washed, an important consideration when white or pale colours were so frequently worn. It could be woven in a variety of textures, shades and patterns and was often embroidered. In Jane Austen's **Northanger Abbey** (1818) the heroine, wondering what to wear for her next ball, 'lay awake ten minutes on Wednesday night debating between her spotted and her tamboured muslin, and nothing but the shortness of the time prevented her buying a new one for the evening'. But the author went on to add, 'it would be mortifying to the feelings of many ladies could they be made

White embroidered muslin dress c.1800.

to understand how little the heart of man is affected by what is costly or new in their attire; how little it is biassed by the texture of their muslin, and how unsusceptible of peculiar tenderness towards the spotted, the sprig, the mull or the jackonet' (all different types of fashionable muslins).

Despite the apparent straightness of the skirt which produced a long column-like silhouette, it was cut with a certain fullness at the back which was extended into a small train for evening wear. This created the required amount of drapery about the limbs.

Although dresses appeared so simple the tight band of the raised waist round the ribcage was probably very uncomfortable. In colder weather a light underdress was often worn beneath a thin gown and long wool or silk shawls were important accessories especially in the evening when a lower neck opening and short sleeves were general. Out of doors a long coat, called a pelisse, cut on similar lines to the dress or a short jacket (a spencer), with long sleeves and a high neck were fashionable.

After about 1810 the mood began to change, moving away from the purely classical taste. By 1815 attempts were being made to alter the unvarying style of women's gowns and very gradually a new line was evolved. Until the early 1820's the waistline remained high but new decorative emphasis on the bodice encouraged it to drop and it eventually regained its natural level in the course of a decade. By 1825 a narrow waist was becoming the focal point and a neat, slim effect was achieved by emphasising the depth of the waistband. Decoration was also applied to the hem of the skirt in the form of flounces and padded bands or rouleaux. The new weight of the hem led to a widening of the skirt and with the adoption of firmer-textured fabrics it began to assume a more triangular and less fluid shape. The skirt continued to widen throughout the 1830's and the fullness was supported by several layers of under-petticoats. In addition, attention was directed towards the sleeves which grew larger and more rounded, reaching their most exaggerated and puffed shape by the mid 1830's. The line of the bodice was fashionably wide across the shoulders and the seam of the sleeve opening dropped over the top of the arm.

To counterbalance the increasing width at the shoulder and hem, women's hair arrangements and head-dresses were enlarged and embellished, sometimes incorporating many yards of ribbon and other ornaments.

Although muslins and fine wools continued to be worn, silk was returning to favour as a dress fabric and more fanciful and colourful patterns were introduced.

The dress of little girls reflected the fashionable line of their mothers' clothes as the bodice lengthened and the skirt and sleeves widened. In the 1820's dresses shortened to reveal the white linen trousers worn by young girls in place of petticoats.

Dress of apricot taffeta overchecked with blue and pink c.1823.

Grey satin wedding dress (worn by a Quaker bride) 1835; man's coat of navy facecloth with strapped trousers 1835-40; child's dress of fine wool 1830-40.

19

A three-piece suit remained the standard wear for men, but in the early years of the century changes were becoming evident. Trousers were introduced – at first for only informal occasions - and they were in general use by 1825, but breeches continued to be worn with evening dress until about 1850. The tail coat, originally a riding coat with the front edges sharply cut away to improve the fall of the coat on horseback, was fashionable day wear until the 1830's, after which it became more usual in the evening. Plain woollen cloths in dark colours had completely replaced the silks of the eighteenth century and now the emphasis was placed on the cut and fit of the coat rather than on surface decoration. Coat, waistcoat and trousers did not necessarily match in colour or material but the general effect was muted.

The frock coat which appeared after 1815, gradually replaced the tail coat for day wear. It was distinguished by its front edges which were cut straight and overlapped rather than being cut away at the sides. In the 1840's the frock coat was tightly fastened at the waist and the skirts appeared rather short and full. For outdoor wear overcoats, cloaks and coats with shoulder capes were made in various weights of cloth. From the beginning of the century the tall-crowned top hat was correct with day clothes (and by the 1840's was also worn with the dress coat at night).

Outdoor wear for women in the mid-nineteenth century consisted mainly in the bonnet and shawl. It was usual for women to cover their heads both indoors and out and in the house all married women wore caps. Deep-brimmed bonnets which framed the face were fashionable in the 1840's and 1850's and these were often made of fine straw, trimmed with ribbon or lace on the underside of the brim. Large veils of fine lace or net could also be attached to the brim.

Shawls had become fashionable in the late-eighteenth century when they were first imported from the East. Indian shawls of fine cashmere wool woven with the traditional pine pattern were particularly sought-after but they became more readily available once they were copied and manufactured at textile centres such as Paisley and Edinburgh in Scotland. The early shawls tended to be oblong but later they became square and increased in size as women's skirts grew wider. The shawl could usefully encompass the increasing width of fashionable dresses without appearing ungainly and it was, in fact, considered to be a very graceful article of clothing. Long overcoats were hardly possible with the prevailing shape of skirt but short capes and sleeved mantles were alternatives to the shawl.

Scene in Great Pulteney Street 1850-60.

Parasols and umbrellas afforded further protection from the weather. Small parasols of silk, sometimes matching the gown were considered essential in the summer. Many had delicately-carved wood or ivory handles and were trimmed with silk fringe, lace or ribbons. Umbrellas had been in use since the early-eighteenth century.

Short ankle boots or 'half-boots' were worn by ladies for walking; they were made with uppers of either leather or a stout cloth and they generally fastened with laces or buttons. Boots for dress wear were black or white satin, with leather soles.

The fashionable image for women of the mid-nineteenth century was very feminine. Small waists, tiny hands and feet and a delicate complexion were much admired. Dresses were intended to look girlish and pretty but at the same time, modest and very ladylike. Soft, pastel colours were popular and it was said in 1851 that 'the Highest Ladies in London are remarkably sensitive about quiet colours, especially out of doors. They have quite a dread of Red and Yellow'. The restricting nature of women's dress at this time encouraged a quiet demeanour, for the dropped shoulder seam, tight bodice, narrow waist and cumbersome skirts prevented much strenuous activity.

Every means possible was used to widen the skirt and the addition of tiered flounces in the late 1840's gave an impression of greater fullness. By 1856 the layers of as many as six under-petticoats were replaced by one foundation garment called the 'artificial crinoline', a bell-shaped petticoat with concentric hoops of flexible steel. Wide skirts were partly designed to make the waist appear small and the waist seam which drew the eye downwards to a long, sharp point at the centre front was another method of creating the illusion of narrowness.

By the early 1860's the perfectly round shape of the skirt was becoming wearisome and moves were made to introduce a more interesting silhouette. The skirt began to be flattened at the front and extended at the back, creating a sweeping, backwards

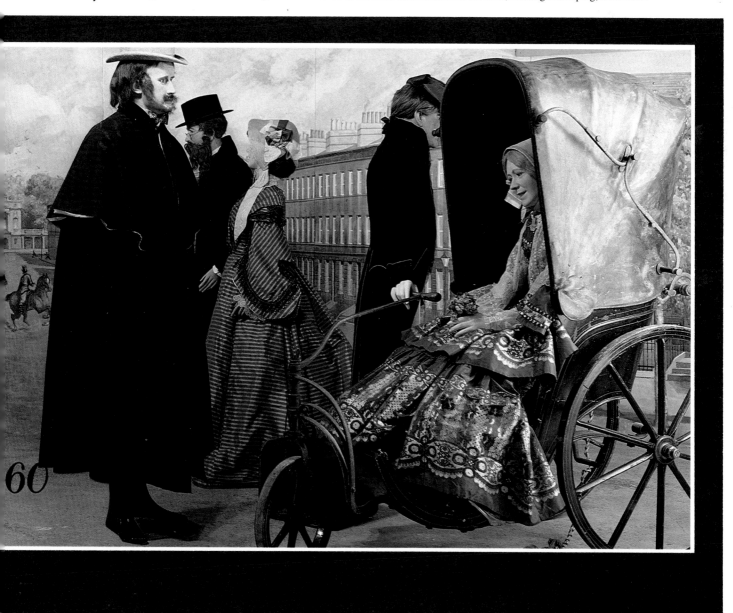

60

movement in the dress; in order to achieve this it was necessary to raise the waistline a few inches. By this time many dresses were made with separate bodices and skirts and few were made entirely by hand since the sewing machine was invented in the early 1850's. The new emphasis on the back included a longer and fuller hair arrangement at the nape of the neck. Sleeves in the 1850's and 1860's widened towards the wrist and were fairly short, to reveal white undersleeves often trimmed with broderie anglaise or lace. These were thought to make the wrists and hands look small and delicate.

The pastel hues of the 1840's and early 1850's began to fade out with the invention of aniline dyes in 1856. New, rather garish colours were introduced and shades such as electric blue, pewter grey and magenta were especially popular. A more strident note became apparent in women's dress as a liking for strong contrasts and bolder decoration emerged; applied black braid or cord, for example, was a fashionable trimming on both adults' and childrens' clothing.

In the last three years of the 1860's the crinoline lost favour and was eventually abandoned. For a short time dresses could be worn without any support but the surplus material at the back of the dress, which almost extended into a train, proved to be unwieldly and soon began to be looped up over the hips. This draped extension to the back of the skirt needed some form of understructure and a support generally known as a 'bustle' was in common use by 1870, giving the dress a distinctive new profile.

By the early 1870's women's dresses were usually made with two skirts, the upper one being shorter and draped over the bustle at the back in soft billowing folds. At the front it formed a draped apron. Flounces were a fashionable form of additional decoration. Attention continued to be focussed on the back of the head and false hair or a chignon was often added.

After 1873 the bustle began to subside and the undulating skirt gradually narrowed and straightened. The bodice became longer and tighter and skirts were tied back inside against the legs with a series of tapes. The fullness at the back of the skirt dropped and had lengthened into a train by 1876. Sleeves were longer and closer fitting and everything tended towards a sheath-like silhouette. In 1876 Paris produced the Princess line, a straight dress with no waist seam which was a fashionable alternative to the separate bodice and skirt. The hair was dressed closer to the head and smaller hats and bonnets were adopted.

Hats were not fashionable at the beginning of the Victorian period (1837–1901) and the bonnet was correct wear with all outdoor dress; but by the late 1840's hats with flat crowns and wide brims were worn for informal occasions. The hat remained an informal accessory to dress until the 1860's when it was worn instead of the bonnet by fashionable younger women. Bonnets continued to be worn with formal day dress until the 1890's.

Day dresses of striped blue silk 1848 and buff silk with matching tippet c.1841.

Day dress of green corded taffeta 1863 and brown watered silk c.1865; girl's mourning dress 1865-70.

In 1880 the general effect of women's dress was very rigid; the waist was tightly constricted and the back of the skirt was quite flat. By 1882, however, the bustle projection had re-emerged and was to have a second life in a new form. Skirts were now supported by the 'crinolette' or 'half-crinoline' which produced an exaggerated shape behind, almost like a bird-cage concealed beneath the dress. Heavy draperies over the hips were also fashionable. The skirt increased in size until 1887, then diminished and the bustle disappeared in 1889.

At this time a new emphasis was placed on the tailoring of dresses made in plain woollen cloth. A fashion for rather mannish clothes – tailor-made coats and skirts worn with masculine collars and ties – made an appearance.

Men themselves adopted much more sombre and uniform clothing in the second half of the nineteenth century, perhaps under the influence of increasing industrialisation. The frock coat was correct wear for all daytime occasions and its sobriety was underlined by its dark grey, blue or black cloth and longer, straigher line. It was often made with a double-breasted fastening but in the late 1870's a single-breasted, high-buttoning style became

(Top) Day dress of cream alpaca trimmed with blue, c. 1872-3.
(Above) A Shawl Shop 1870-80.

more usual. Trousers were cut straight and rather long and had no centre crease or turn-ups until the late 1890's. Waistcoats and neckties could provide a certain amount of colour and individuality in the male suit, however, and there was a revival of fancy waistcoats with woven or embroidered patterns in the 1890's.

After 1889 the shape of women's dress softened and loosened; the hem of the skirt widened and a little fullness appeared at the head of the sleeve, gradually expanding during the early 1890's. The bodice also developed a small stand collar.

Once the bustle was abandoned the skirt fitted closer over the hips and the waist looked less obviously narrow. Other means of making the waist appear small were exploited and the enlarged shoulders and gored skirts of the 1890's were used to this end. By 1895 the upper sleeve was very large and full, giving the

The Conservatory 1880-90.

24

dress a marked horizontal emphasis which was balanced by the width of the skirt at the hem and a much rounder style of dressing the hair. Large hats became very fashionable.

The traditional dress for weddings – a white gown, veil and orange blossom – dates from the Victorian period. White was worn at weddings in earlier periods but even in the nineteenth century it was not invariable; coloured dresses were often worn by older brides, widows or those in mourning. It was customary to wear the dress for some time afterwards as an evening or best dress so for poorer brides a coloured dress was more serviceable. It was always made with a train and was often trimmed with artificial orange blossom which became fashionable in the 1830's. Veils were not generally worn until the nineteenth century and Queen Victoria seems to have been the first English royal bride to do so. They were always white and usually of lace (Brussels and Honiton laces were particularly popular). At first they did not cover the face and they were generally worn with a wreath of orange blossom. Some brides preferred to wear a bonnet with a veil attached, especially if it was to be a quiet wedding.

A Bedroom 1890-1900 (Wedding dress 1895).

Underwear

The garments worn next to the skin or beneath the upper clothes play an important role in the development of fashion. They provide a foundation for all the main items of dress and contribute to the general shape and effect of any costume.

Underclothes have two principal functions, one to serve as a hygienic and comfortable layer between the skin and main body garments and secondly, to create the shape of fashion by restricting or enlarging the natural contours of the human figure. The first category includes underlinen such as shirts, chemises, vests and drawers; the second – which is often termed 'structural underwear' – includes stays, corsets, hoop-petticoats, crinolines, bustles and other dress supports.

Eighteenth-century stays were made from several layers of stout linen or cotton stitched together and inserted with strips of whalebone. A long, flat piece of wood (or whalebone, horn or ivory) called a 'busk' was also

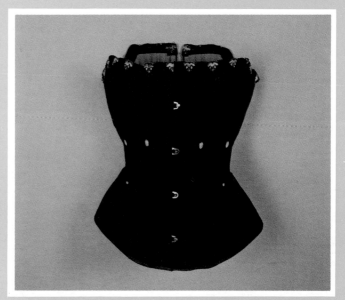

(Above) Woman's corset of black alpaca 1890-95.
(Right) Woman's corset of brown twill 1775-80.

slipped down the centre front to keep it rigid. Shoulder straps kept the garment in place and it was fastened by lacing through eyelet holes. After the mid-nineteenth century front-fastening and strapless corsets with shaped gussets over the breasts and hips were adopted. Stocking suspenders were not attached until the 1890's. Corsets were worn by all women and were considered an essential part of dress until the last quarter of the nineteenth century.

An unusual novelty, on display in the Museum of Costume, are the 'Patriotic' corsets made during the 1914–1918 War, displaying the colours and flags of various countries.

It was customary to cover the corset with a short under-bodice which was known at different times as a corset cover, petticoat-bodice or camisole.

Corsets were never worn next to the skin and until the 1920's were always put on over a shift or chemise. Since at least the Middle Ages it has been usual for men and women to wear a layer of underlinen in the form of a shirt or – in the case of women – a full-length, sleeved chemise. Originally both garments were similar in cut, basically T-shaped and loose fitting, made in the tunic style (that is they passed over the head as opposed to fastening up the centre front like a coat).

The most popular material for underclothes was linen because it washed well and felt pleasant next to the skin. Wool and silk have been used but they are less pratical, not being so easy to wash nor as hard-wearing. During the nineteenth century cotton became more widely used for undergarments but for some time it was considered a socially inferior alternative to linen. The use of nylon and other man-made fibres for underwear is a fairly recent (though very significant) development and these were not manufactured on a wide scale until the 1950's.

An underlayer of linen not only preserved the upper garments from soiling but also protected the skin from being chafed or rubbed by outer clothes – an important consideration in periods when stiff silks, heavy woollen cloths and fur linings were fashionable. It is evident that most men and women possessed several changes of underlinen so shirts and chemises could be washed frequently. Although baths were less usual until the nineteenth century, people were, in fact, much cleaner than is generally thought and the idea of wearing upper garments (such as dresses, trousers and sweaters) next to the skin as we do today would have shocked earlier generations.

Bustle 1880-85.

Crinolette 1875-80.

By the early nineteenth centry the male shirt was a voluminous, thigh-length garment with cuffed sleeves and a deep neckband. Until the 1860's the neckband or collar was worn upright but then it became acceptable to turn down the collar over the necktie with informal wear. The upright, wing or butterfly collar has continued to be worn with very formal evening dress (with a white bow tie and tail coat) to the present day. The vertical slit forming the centre front opening was not usually fastened with buttons or studs until the early nineteenth century; before then the opening was concealed by a pleated or gathered ruffle attached to one edge and was visible just above the waistcoat when a man was fully dressed.

Petticoats have played an important part in supporting or creating the shape of women's skirts. When full skirts returned to fashion in the nineteenth century one or more waist-petticoats were worn and by the 1840's as many as six were usual. These varied in texture and appearance, the uppermost petticoat being lighter and more decorative with the addition of tucks, embroidery or broderie anglaise. Beneath this, a stiff horsehair petticoat was worn to give the skirt its required width. It was made from linen woven with horsehair and the term 'crinoline' petticoat is derived from the French 'crin' (horsehair) and 'lin' (linen). By the early 1850's it was impossible to add any more layers and skirts were very cumbersome until the invention of the 'artificial' crinoline petticoat.

The artifcial crinoline was a round petticoat or frame into which were inserted graduated hoops of cane, whalebone or – after 1856 – thin, flexible steels. This immediately dispensed with all except one petticoat and provided the perfect support for wide skirts. It was light, easy and comfortable to wear and swung out attractively as a woman walked, though there were many jokes in **Punch** about the inconvenience of crinolines in confined spaces.

Skirts reached their maximum width in the 1860's but by 1863 the shape had altered to become flatter at the front and longer at the back. In 1867 the crinoline passed abruptly out of fashion, probably because it was now viewed with almost universal boredom and for about two years skirts were worn with little or no support.

Corset cover, petticoat, crinoline, pocket, drawers 1850-60.

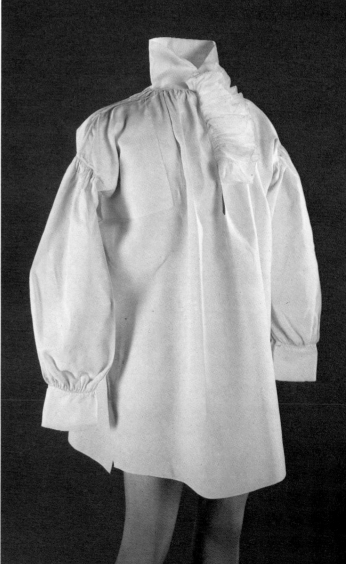

Man's linen shirt 1830-40.

By the early 1870's, however, women's dresses required some kind of under-structure to improve the drapery of the full skirt at the back. Various devices such as half-crinolines, pads, stiff frills of horsehair cloth or small wire frames were adopted and these were known as 'dress improvers', 'tournures' or 'bustles'. The bustle had two lives: it was fashionable between about 1870 and 1876 and then from about 1882 to 1889 (but in its second phase it was more exaggerated in shape).

During the second half of the century cotton was more often used for women's underwear and more decoration was applied to garments. By the end of the century white embroidery, insertions of lace, ornamental tucks and other trimmings were usual and during the Edwardian period (1901–10) women's underwear became particularly luxurious.

Drawers for women were not general until the 1840's when they consisted of two tubular legs on a waistband, with the inside seams left open. Seamed legs on drawers appeared in the 1880's and combinations (combining a chemise and drawers) were adopted in the second half of the 1870's when tight fitting tie-back dresses became fashionable.

Stockings of knitted cotton or silk were usually black or white in the nineteenth century (though coloured stockings were fashionable in the 1860's and 1870's). White was correct with evening dress but black stockings were worn with black dresses and almost always in the daytime by the end of the century. Throughout the period they could be ornamented with decorative clocks or openwork and embroidery over the instep. Flesh-coloured stockings were generally adopted after the hemline shortened in 1914. Nylon stockings made their first appearance in America in 1938 but were not widely available in this country until the early 1950's.

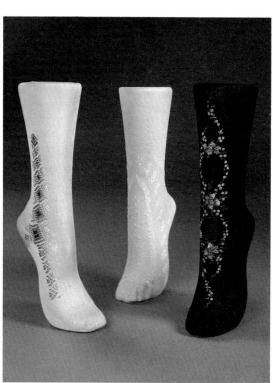

Embroidered stockings c.1800; c.1840; 1880-90.

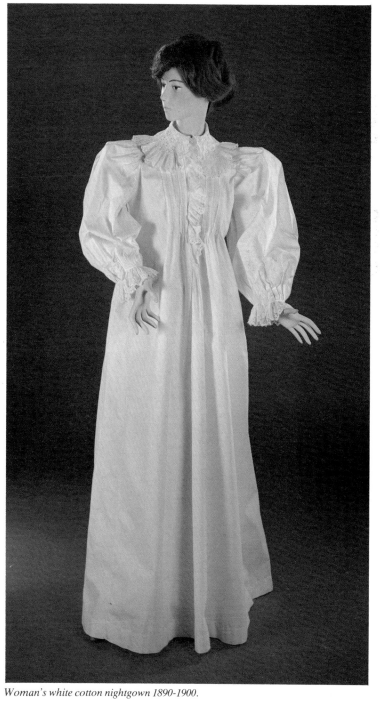

Woman's white cotton nightgown 1890-1900.

29

20th Century Fashion

Queen Victoria's death in January 1901 heralded the beginning of a new reign as well as a new century. The dress of the Edwardian period (1901–1910) however, did not differ significantly from that of the late-Victorian era. The frock coat was still correct formal day wear for men and strict social conventions hardly relaxed before the outbreak of the First World War. In women's dress waists were still small and the 'S'-bend shape of figure, achieved by tightly-laced corsets, was the fashionable silhouette. An ideal image of the period was the 'Gibson Girl', so-called after the paintings and drawings by the American artist Charles Dana Gibson (and his wife Irene, one of the beautiful Langhorne sisters, was the source of his inspiration). A tall, rather statuesque impression was given by the clothes and under-garments worn by women during the decade. A fullness at the front of the bodice and at the back of the skirt not only diminished the apparent size of the waist but also created the illusion of curves which was echoed by the sweeping line of the wide-hemmed skirt. Necks were made to appear longer by the deep neckband of the bodice and the hair was dressed out in a very soft, full style. Large hats, which were sometimes tilted to one side, also increased the height of the figure.

Pastel colours (such as lavender, primrose, eau-de-nil and old rose) and white were immensely popular and delicate dress fabrics were profusely trimmed with lace, chiffon, net and ribbons.

After 1910 these elements disappeared to be replaced, in time, by a new simplicity of appearance and economy in design and cut. A revival of the early-nineteenth century 'Directoire' style with the short-waisted bodice brought back a tubular-shaped skirt; tight lacing was at last abandoned and there was a move away from the curvaceous silhouette. Bolder colours were adopted and the trimming of women's dress was more disciplined, with carefully placed accents (often in the form of buttons or applied braid and cord). The simplicity of the slim, straight skirt was deceptive, nevertheless, because its narrowness round the ankles made walking extremely difficult and it was aptly known as the 'hobble' skirt.

On the eve of the 1914–1918 World War a more utilitarian form of dress for women was beginning to emerge. By 1913 the first moves towards a raising of the hemline became apparent; once war broke out and the services of

(Above) Striped chiffon day dress c.1907.
(Right) Boys's sailor suit c.1914; woman's dress c.1916; Lieutenant's uniform (Bedfordshire Regiment) 1914-18.

women were required for the war effort the shorter skirt was hastened in. The new length, which revealed the ankles, was a revolutionary step because women had been wearing full-length skirts since the time of the Ancient Greeks but it was probably accepted more easily than most new fashions because of the distractions and necessities of the war. As the skirt shortened the hem widened and by 1916, dresses with full skirts were well established. The high waistline gradually dropped and was nearing its natural level by 1920.

Women's clothes of the 1920's are usually associated with a distinctive style: the loose chemise-dress, often with a waist dropped to hip level, short skirts, short hair, deep-brimmed cloche hats and bandeaux worn low over the forehead in the evening. In the early years of the decade the hemline was still fairly long, it gradually shortened after 1924 to reach its highest level, just covering the knee-cap, in 1927. The waistline dropped fairly rapidly but until 1922 waists at the normal level or a little higher were still to be seen. The desirable figure was completely flat and the tube-like shapeless dresses were designed to conceal all natural contours; foundation garments were made to flatten the bust and hips.

Shorter skirts drew attention to the legs and feet and after 1915 heels were worn higher. In the 1920's the usual black or white stockings of earlier decades were replaced by flesh-coloured hose and sometimes coloured stockings to match the dress for evening wear.

Short bobbed hair was very popular and, in fact, it became increasingly difficult to wear long hair pinned up with the close-fitting, helmet-shaped hats that were so fashionable. Cosmetics were more generally accepted and widely used during the period.

The flat surface and plain areas of colour created by the rectangular chemise-dress presented problems to the designers and it was soon felt necessary to decorate dresses for evening or formal wear. One of the most popular forms of decoration was bead embroidery on fine net or silk fabrics. Some of these dresses are works of art in their own right and would have come to life when worn; with movement and the play of reflected light on the glass beads the dresses presented an almost kaleidoscopic effect of pattern and colour.

Bead-embroidered evening dress by Callot Soeurs, Paris, 1923.

A Sitting Room 1920-1930.

Men's clothes were becoming much less formal and more comfortable by the 1920's. After the First World War many of the rigid social rules of the Edwardian period were abandoned and, in particular, the frock coat and top hat for day wear disappeared. The lounge suit had been slowly becoming a more acceptable alternative to the frock and morning coats since the 1890's and could now be worn for most daytime functions. In 1925 trousers with wider legs (popularly known as 'Oxford Bags') came into fashion and shoulders became a little squarer to balance the new width.

During the inter-war years it remained usual for men to dress in the evening. The formal version of men's evening dress consisted of a tail coat with matching trousers in a fine woollen cloth, either black or very dark blue in colour, worn with a white waistcoat (piqué cotton or marcella), a starched dress shirt, stiff wing collar, white bow tie and black patent leather shoes. Outdoor accessories included a top hat (usually called a silk hat), white kid gloves, walking stick and opera cloak or evening overcoat. The less formal version of the suit, worn for private dinners, the theatre or concerts was the dinner jacket (cut on the lines of the lounge coat) with evening trousers, black waistcoat and black bow tie.

Long dresses for evening functions were usual for women in the 1930's. During the decade the cut of both day and evening dresses was skilfully developed and the designer Madeleine Vionnet was famous for her expertise in the bias cut. Cutting the dress fabric on the cross grain (or bias) gave the couturier or dressmaker more opportunity for moulding and draping the material which has a more elastic quality on the diagonal. 1930's dresses were made to fit closely over the bust and hips and flare out smoothly at the hem. This new line had begun to emerge at the very end of the 1920's when women became bored with the uncompromising and geometrical shape of fashionable dresses. By 1930 a return to the more natural shape and curves of the female figure was increasingly evident; the waistline was restored to the normal position, the bust was

Gold embroidered velvet evening dress and jacket by Elsa Schiaparelli 1938; man in full evening dress 1930-40.

Day dress of blue and white georgette c. 1935.

no longer obliterated and the hemline was considerably lengthened. The most suitable dress fabrics were soft and fluid so that silk crêpe-de-chine and chiffon were particularly popular.

One of the most important dress designers of the decade was Elsa Schiaparelli whose clothes were noted for their vivacity and originality especially in the late 1930's when it was chic to be 'amusing'. She worked with some of the most advanced artists of her day and many of her clothes included contemporary surrealist motifs (such as a hat shaped like a shoe or a dress patterned with lifelike lobsters and sprigs of parsley).

With the outbreak of the Second World War in 1939 British fashion virtually came to a standstill and did not revive until after 1945. The rationing of cloth and clothing was introduced in 1941 and utility regulations severely restricted the production of new styles.

In the interests of economy hems were made as short as was thought possible (to the knee) and the width of the skirt was reduced. Shoulders, however, were padded to a very square shape (a trend which had begun in 1935) giving dresses and especially suits a masculine air. Practical shoes with rounded toes, low heels and thick soles were also worn. Hairstyles allowed some scope for variety and femininity and they became rather long and curled.

War-time conditions – air-raids and petrol rationing – curtailed social activities and it was sometimes impractical to wear full evening dress. Women were often obliged to wear the same clothes all day and found it useful to adopt short evening dresses, a war-time innovation.

Although most men were serving in the armed forces, uniforms and civilian suits were also affected by utility regulations. In order to save material waistcoats, pockets and trouser turn-ups were frequently omitted from the suit and good cloth was difficult to find. At the end of the war the de-mobilized forces were issued with mass-produced 'De-mob' suits cut on similar utility lines in the style of the late 1930's which seemed rather shapeless and old-fashioned by 1945. A few years later, when men began to buy new suits again and the country was recovering from war, there was a renewed interest in fashion amongst younger men. By 1950 more elegant, dark suits, cut on narrower lines were being worn with white shirts and slightly longer hair.

The end of the war also brought a revival of fashion for women although clothes did not change immediately (rationing in Britain lasted in one form or another until 1949). There was a longing for more colour and dresses with greater fullness and length. When Christian Dior introduced his 'New Look' collection in 1947 it caused an immediate sensation. The square, solid look of previous years was swept away in favour of a softly rounded shoulder, tightly emphasized waist and a very wide, long skirt (held out by several layers of petticoats). At the same time lighter and higher-heeled shoes returned to general wear.

Dior continued to be influential during the 1950's although Balenciaga was probably the most significant designer of the decade.

Printed crêpe-de-chine dress 1940.

Woman's suit by Christian Dior 1947; man's suit 1948.

33

Both introduced new shapes in women's clothes, often distorting the natural lines of the figure with, for example, balloon-shaped dresses and coats with cocoon-like curves, the tunic dress and the return of the high waist for a short time. John Cavanagh's evening dress of 1958 in the Museum of Costume illustrates the vogue for cutting evening dresses shorter at the front than at the back and the great popularity of strapless bodices (firmly boned to support the gown). As Britain recovered from the war fashion in this country began to flourish with the work of designers such as Norman Hartnell, Hardy Amies, Digby Morton, Victor Stiebel and Charles Creed.

In the early 1950's the prevailing look for women was extremely neat, tailored and well-groomed. Hair cut short and dressed close to the head, formal hats with small veils and high-heeled court shoes contributed to this appearance, although casual wear, especially for younger women, was becoming more widespread. Trousers (strictly for informal occasions) and separates were increasingly popular.

The 1960's was a decade of great change and, in some respects, of revolution. For young people it was a period of experiment and progress, now made possible after the long years of re-adjustment following the war. The abolition of national service, government grants for higher education and a more affluent society resulted in greater freedom and opportunity for the young. For the first time clothes began to be designed by the young, specifically for the young and London in particular emerged as a new centre of original and exciting fashion. Mary Quant is perhaps the best known designer who produced cheap but attractive clothes intended solely for young women and it is significant that hers was the first outfit chosen as the 'Dress of the Year' when the Museum of Costume opened in 1963.

The outfit represents several of the new ideas to emerge at this time. A simpler, sharper (almost spiky) line had already developed with the slimmer 'A' line dresses and skirts worn with pointed-toed shoes and high stiletto heels. The hemline rose to knee-length in 1963 and then well above the knee in following years. The mini-skirt reached its shortest length in 1967 when it rose to the level of the thighs. Such short skirts at first appeared revolutionary since even in

Ball gown in pink acetate and lurex brocade by John Cavanagh 1958.

Grey shift dress and cream chiffon blouse by Mary Quant 1963 (the first 'Dress of the Year').

the 1920's the hem had never risen above the knee. Two new accessories to dress were long boots and tights which replaced stockings at the end of the 1960's (having become almost essential with the miniscule skirts). Short-skirted, simple shift dresses of the later 1960's brought back a squarer line while boots and shoes developed blunt toes and stubby heels. Hair was ideally flat and straight and worn increasingly long (wigs and hair pieces were back in fashion by 1964). A liking for plain colours, clear contrasts and a general absence of ornament underlined the geometrical shape of women's dress which was taken a step further by the 'space age' or 'couture future' clothes of the French designer Courrèges in 1967. Trousers and trouser suits were worn everywhere, in the daytime and in the evening.

By 1970 a reaction against the uncompromising lines of later-1960's fashions had already set in. Longer, wider skirts and trousers were introduced in 1968, the midi-and maxi-length coats appeared in 1969 and a layered look began to break up the prevailing line.

Two trends appear to have characterized the 1970's. On the one hand, clothes looked forwards and adapted themselves to current life-styles; mass-production and the continuing development of man-made fibres have made practical comfortable and relatively inexpensive clothes available to everyone. A greater informality in dress (for both men and women) dispensed with many of the old rules and the need to wear specific clothes for different occasions. On the other hand, fashion also looked backwards, there was a conscious rejection of contemporary influences and a nostalgia for the dress of the past, of other countries or ways of life, resulting in many 'romantic' and sometimes impractical forms of clothing. There were revivals of fashions, for example, from the Edwardian period (notably in the work of Laura Ashley), from the 1930's and the 1940's; exotic or ethnic clothes, especially from the East, were popular and many elements of working, sporting or country dress were taken up into fashionable wear (apart from the already well-established denim jeans).

The work of some of the most distinguished contemporary dress designers is represented in the Museum's collections and these include Jean Muir, Bill Gibb, Zandra Rhodes, Gina Fratini, John Bates and Jap.

Evening dress and coat of black and white ostrich feathers by Yves St. Laurent 1964.

Men's clothes by Cerruti ('Clothes of the Year' 1978) and outfit by Jeff Sayre 1979.

Royal & Ceremonial Clothes

The Museum of Costume has in its collections a number of clothes belonging to the British Royal family and there are items on display worn by Queen Victoria, Queen Alexandra, Queen Mary and Queen Elizabeth the Queen Mother.

Day clothes worn by Queen Victoria include a tartan woollen croquet skirt and petticoat 1855–60; the under-petticoat is of cream lawn with an edging of broderie anglaise at the hem. Croquet was an extremely popular outdoor game for men and women at this date.

A dress, consisting of a separate bodice and skirt, in black corded silk of the late 1880's was also worn by Queen Victoria and is typical of the sombre clothes she adopted for mourning after the death of Prince Albert in 1861.

Most of the garments belonging to Queen Alexandra in the Museum were worn by her when she was Princess of Wales and several date from the 1890's. On display is an evening dress (again, a separate bodice and skirt) of lilac watered silk trimmed with toning velvet and cream lace. This was made for her by Morin Blossier of Paris in 1893.

Two other royal evening dresses, of the present century, illustrate the use of bead embroidery for formal clothes. An evening dress with matching three-quarter length coat worn by Queen Mary in about 1930 is worked with black and purple-shaded sequins and is trimmed with black foxaline. Norman Hartnell is perhaps most famous for the bead-embroidered dresses designed for the Royal family and one worn by the Queen Mother in 1954 is an excellent example of his work.

Lilac watered silk evening dress worn by Queen Alexandra (when Princess of Wales) 1893.

Croquet skirt in Royal Victoria tartan worn by Queen Victoria 1855-60.

Coronets of silver gilt, crimson velvet and ermine.

At Court and for special occasions such as Coronations and the State Opening of Parliament, speical clothes have been worn by Peers of the Realm, officials and dignitaries. Robes and coronets worn by the Peers at a Coronation are distinguished by certain features according to the degree of rank. The coronets of silver gilt and crimson velvet trimmed with ermine and a gold tassel, for example, have different numbers of 'pearls' or silver balls set on the rim some of which alternate with strawberry leaves; some pearls are raised on points. The black spots or 'doublets' of ermine tails on the fur also refer to rank. The coronets of peeresses are much smaller than those of the peers and are made to sit on top of the head (secured

Bead-embroidered satin evening dress by Norman Hartnell, belonging to Queen Elizabeth the Queen Mother.

equinned evening dress and coat worn by Queen Mary c.1930.

by combs) rather than encircling the brow.
Examples of the coronets worn by a Baron,
Baroness, Earl, Marchioness, Viscount and
Viscountess are illustrated here.

A peer's robes consist of a crimson velvet cloak,
open at the front, edged with miniver, with a cape of
miniver spotted with rows of black ermine tails.

A peeress's robes are different, having short close-fitting
sleeves edged with miniver and long trains (the length of
which alters with rank); in addition the front edges do not
meet but otherwise the colour and material are similar to
peers' robes.

Members of the Order of the Garter – the oldest surviving order
of Chivalry in Europe – also wear their own robes and insignia on
State occasions. The garter itself is made of dark blue velvet one inch
wide, edged with gold and embroidered with the motto of the order
'Honi soit qui Mal y Pense' ('Let shame be to him who thinks Evil'). The
Star shown here is an eight-pointed star of chipped silver the centre of
which bears the cross of St George encircled by a blue enamel garter. The
Star was always worn on the left breast of full-dress uniform, court dress or
full evening dress.

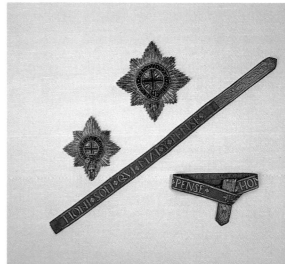

Garters and Stars of the Order of the Garter.

Man's velvet court suit with miniature medals 1907.

Marchioness's robe and train 1900.

Dolls & Toys

Most of the dolls and toys in the Museum's collection date from the nineteenth and twentieth centuries when they were mass-produced on a wide scale and with increasing sophistication. Small figures and miniature items for children were, however, produced in much earlier periods. Many playthings were designed primarily for children but must also have delighted adults.

By the seventeenth century a wide variety of toys were available for children and in the eighteenth century a number of different dolls were produced, such as carved wooden figures, dolls with wax heads and stuffed rag dolls. Some of these were very finely and expensively dressed. Dolls' houses (or 'Baby Houses' as they were known in England) also became very popular.

Wax-headed dolls 1860 and 1867.

A great number of toy-making firms flourished in Europe and America during the nineteenth century; France and Gemany were particularly prominent in the manufacturer of wax and porcelain-headed dolls but some fin examples were also made in England.

Simple, jointed wooden dolls (popularly called 'wooden tops') continued to be made but there was a continual demand for more life-like heads (which were attached to a body consisting of a series of rectangular-shaped bags filled with sawdust). The wax head were made in several different ways; some were made entirely of wax (poured in layers into a mould) others had a composition cast dipped into wax and another method, popular at th end of the nineteenth century, was to pour a layer of plaster into a wax mould. Glass eyes were inserted and the eyebrows and lips painted on to the face. Hair was attached either by implanting into the wax head (for high quality dolls) or through a hole in the centre of the crown eyelashes could also be implanted in the wax. Occasionally real hair was used but as a rule it was mohair. The sleeping eye mechanism worked by a lead counterweight was a German innovation and voice boxes were often inserted.

Porcelain heads were extensively made in the Victorian period and, again, there were several different types such as bisque (an unglazed porcelain) and parian ware. Some heads were made of papier maché and after 1850 various composition substances were tried. The fragile nature of wax and porcelain was a continua problem but many of the substitutes introduced were, in the long run, unsuccessful. Rubber, for example, tended to dry up and crack while the paint on tin heads frequently chipped.

Golliwogs and Teddy Bears date from the early years of this century. The golliwog was a character invented by Florence Upton in her book **The Adventures of Two Dutch Dolls and a Golliwog** in 1895 but it became popular as a soft toy a few years later. The Teddy Bear appeared in 1903; it is believed that the first was made by an American toymaker who copied a bear cub in a cartoon of the politician, Theodore (Teddy) Roosevelt. The early bears differ from modern versions in having long, pointed noses and small ears.

Other popular toys to be seen here include dolls' houses and miniature furniture, toy soldiers and farm animals, card games and puzzles, a rocking horse, dolls' prams and a variety of children's books.

Dolls' tea party 1860-1910.

French musical doll with china head 1880—90.